Dream Big

and
Imagine the
Nearly Impossible

Creative Journal for Teens

Activinotes

Activinotes

DAILY JOURNALS, PLANNERS, NOTEBOOKS AND OTHER BLANK BOOKS

journal

Smile

CHEER UP

nothing is impossible

Dream Big!

Quotes

Thoughts to ponder

notes:

journal

Smile

CHEER
UP

nothing is impossible

Dream
Big!

Quotes

Thoughts to ponder

notes:

journal

Smile

CHEER
UP

nothing is impossible

Dream Big!

Quotes

Thoughts to ponder

notes:

journal

Smile

CHEER UP!

nothing is impossible

Dream Big!

Quotes

Thoughts to ponder

notes:

journal

Smile

CHEER UP

nothing is impossible

Dream Big!

notes

Thoughts to ponder

notes:

journal

Smile

CHEER UP

nothing is impossible

Dream Big!

Quotes

Thoughts to ponder

notes:

journal

Smile

CHEER
UP

nothing is
impossible

Dream
Big!

Quotes

Thoughts to ponder

notes:

journal

Smile

CHEER
UP

nothing is impossible

Dream Big!

quotes

Thoughts to ponder

notes:

journal

Smile

CHEER UP

nothing is impossible

Dream Big!

notes

Thoughts to ponder

notes:

 journal

 Smile

 CHEER UP

 nothing is impossible

 Dream Big!

Quotes

Thoughts to ponder

notes:

journal

Smile

CHEER
UP

nothing is impossible

Dream
Big!

Quotes

Thoughts to ponder

notes:

journal

Smile

CHEER UP

nothing is impossible

Dream Big!

quotes

Thoughts to ponder

notes:

journal

Smile

CHEER UP

nothing is impossible

Dream Big!

Quotes

Thoughts to ponder

notes:

journal

Smile

CHEER UP

nothing is impossible

Dream Big!

Quotes

Thoughts to ponder

notes:

journal

Smile

CHEER UP

nothing is impossible

Dream Big!

quotes

Thoughts to ponder

notes:

journal

Smile

CHEER UP

nothing is impossible

Dream Big!

Quotes

Thoughts to ponder

notes:

journal

Smile

CHEER UP

nothing is impossible

Dream Big!

quotes

Thoughts to ponder

notes:

journal

Smile

nothing is impossible

Dream Big!

Quotes

Thoughts to ponder

notes:

journal

Smile

CHEER UP

nothing is impossible

Dream Big!

Quotes

Thoughts to ponder

notes:

journal

Smile

CHEER UP

nothing is impossible

Dream Big!

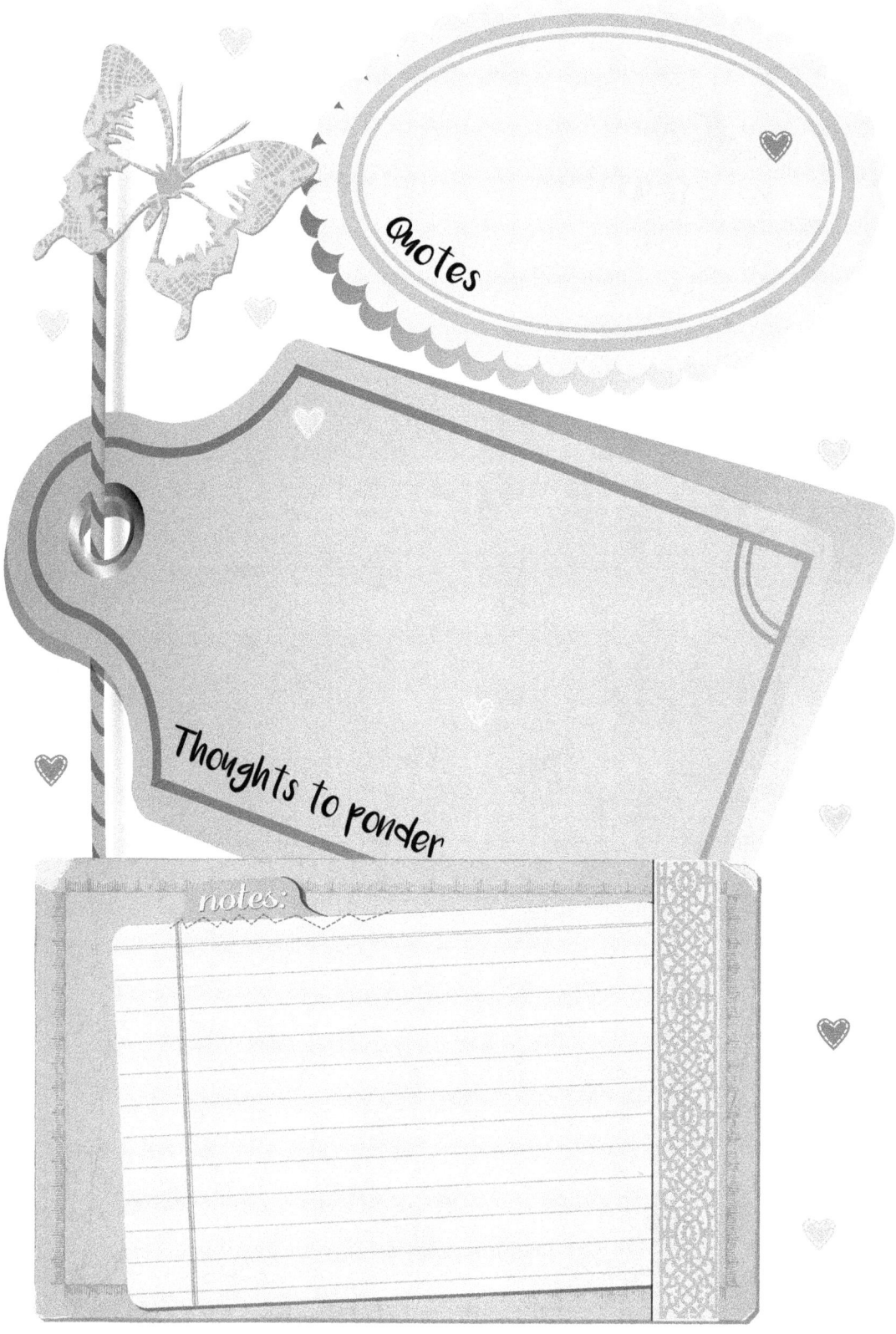

Quotes

Thoughts to ponder

notes:

journal

Smile

CHEER UP

nothing is impossible

Dream Big!

Quotes

Thoughts to ponder

notes:

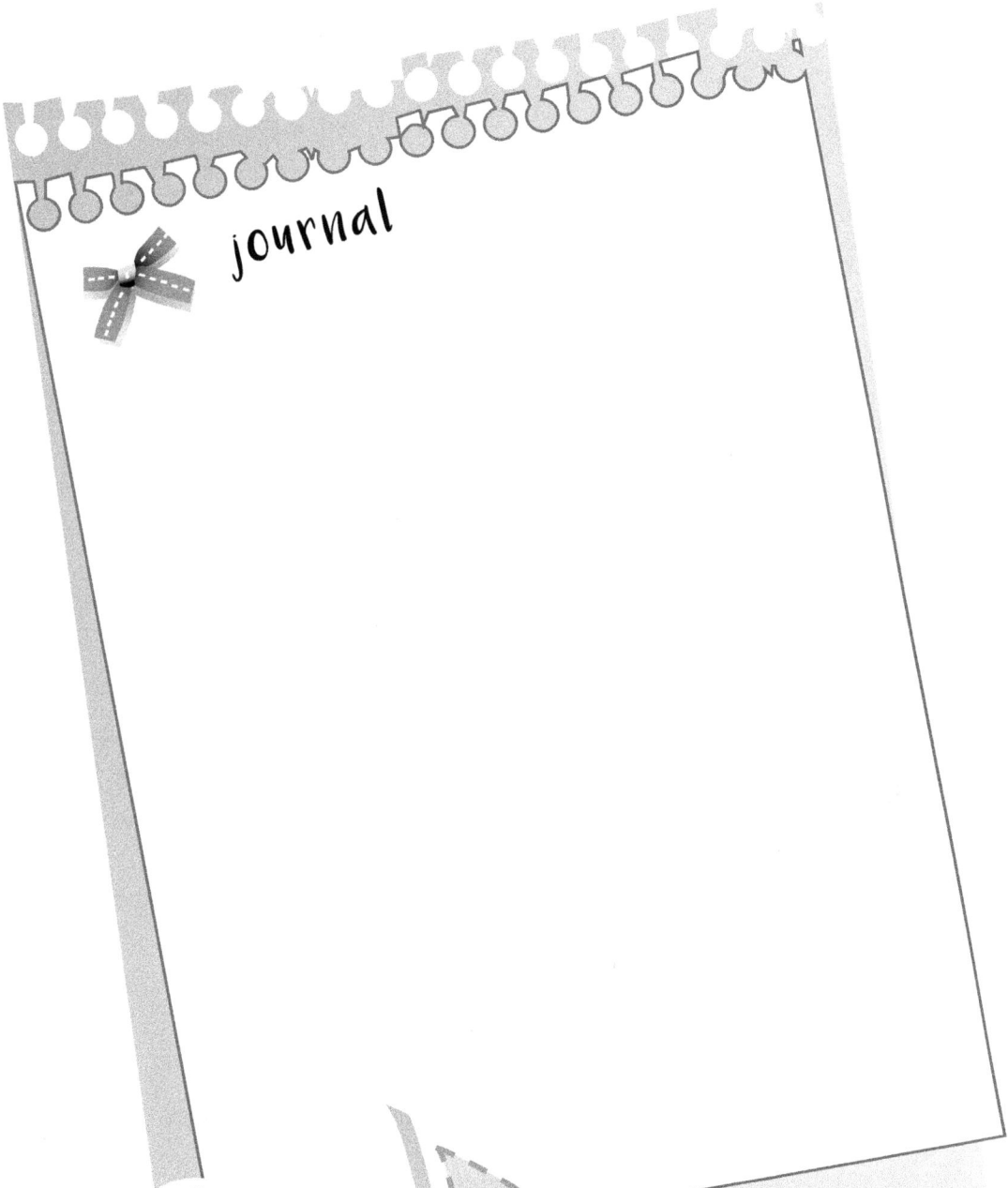

journal

Smile

CHEER
UP

nothing is impossible

Dream Big!

Quotes

Thoughts to ponder

notes:

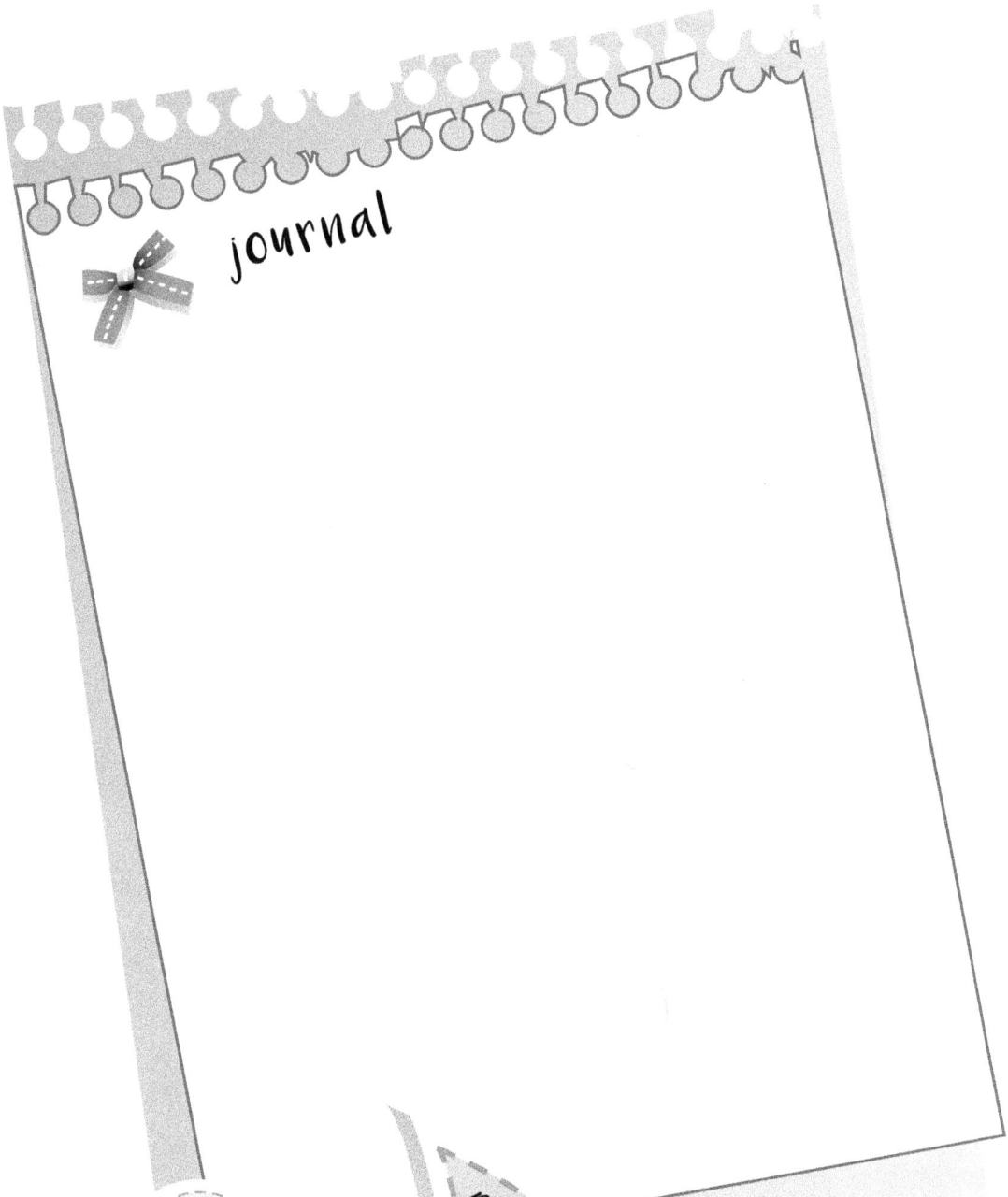

journal

Smile

CHEER
UP

nothing is impossible

Dream Big!

notes

Thoughts to ponder

notes:

journal

Smile

CHEER UP

nothing is impossible

Dream Big!

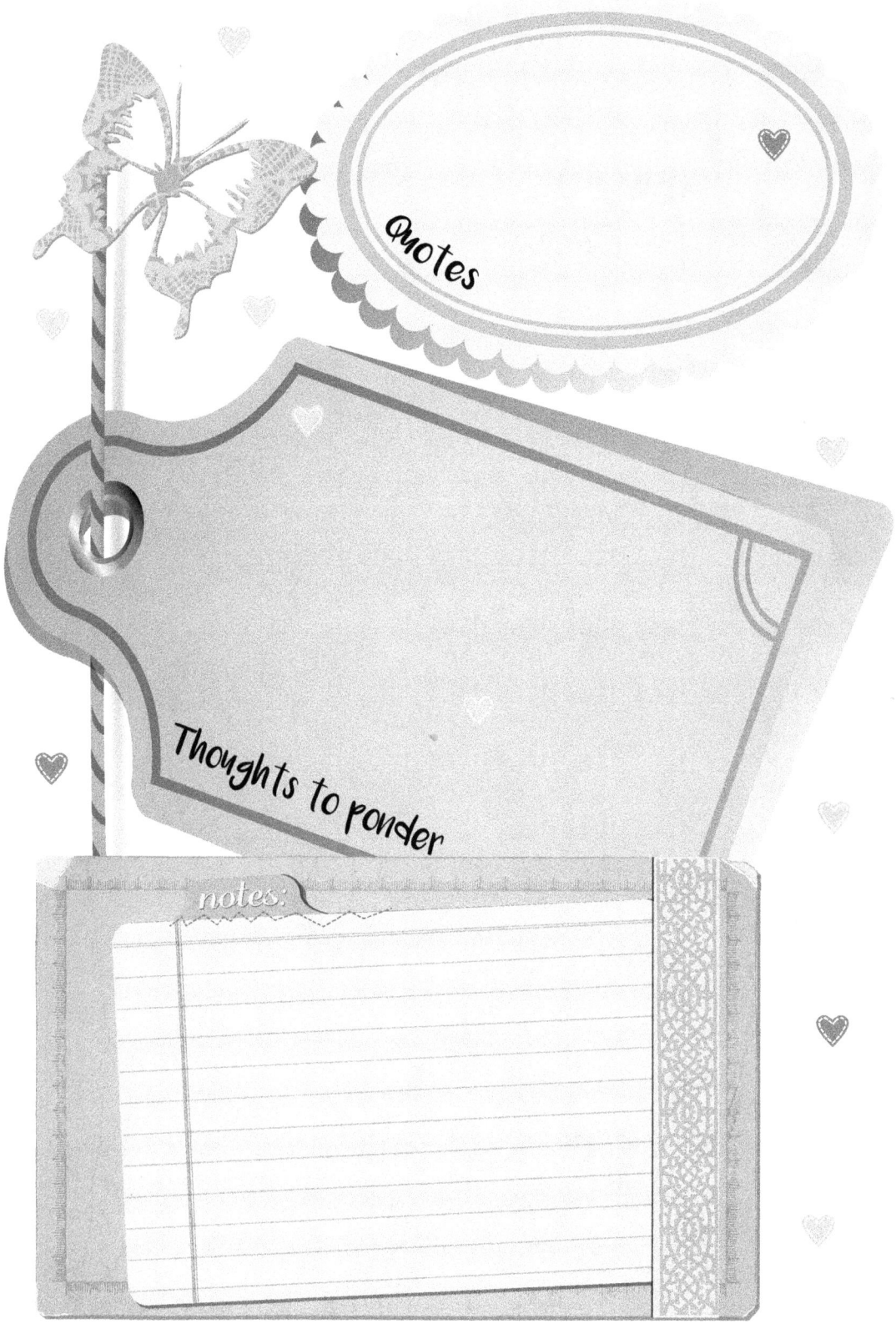

Quotes

Thoughts to ponder

notes:

journal

Smile

nothing is impossible

Dream Big!

Quotes

Thoughts to ponder

notes:

 journal

 Smile

 CHEER UP

 nothing is impossible

 Dream Big!

Quotes

Thoughts to ponder

notes:

journal

Smile

CHEER UP!

nothing is impossible

Dream Big!

notes

Thoughts to ponder

notes:

 journal

 Smile

 CHEER UP

 nothing is impossible

 Dream Big!

Quotes

Thoughts to ponder

notes:

journal

Smile

CHEER UP!

nothing is impossible

Dream Big!

Quotes

Thoughts to ponder

notes:

journal

Smile

CHEER
UP

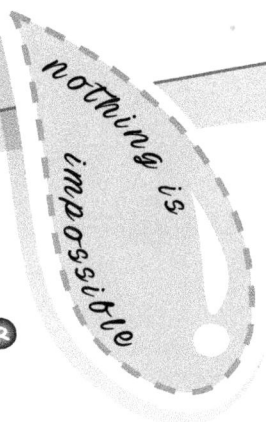

nothing is
impossible

Dream
Big!

Quotes

Thoughts to ponder

notes:

journal

Smile

CHEER UP

nothing is impossible

Dream Big!

Quotes

Thoughts to ponder

notes:

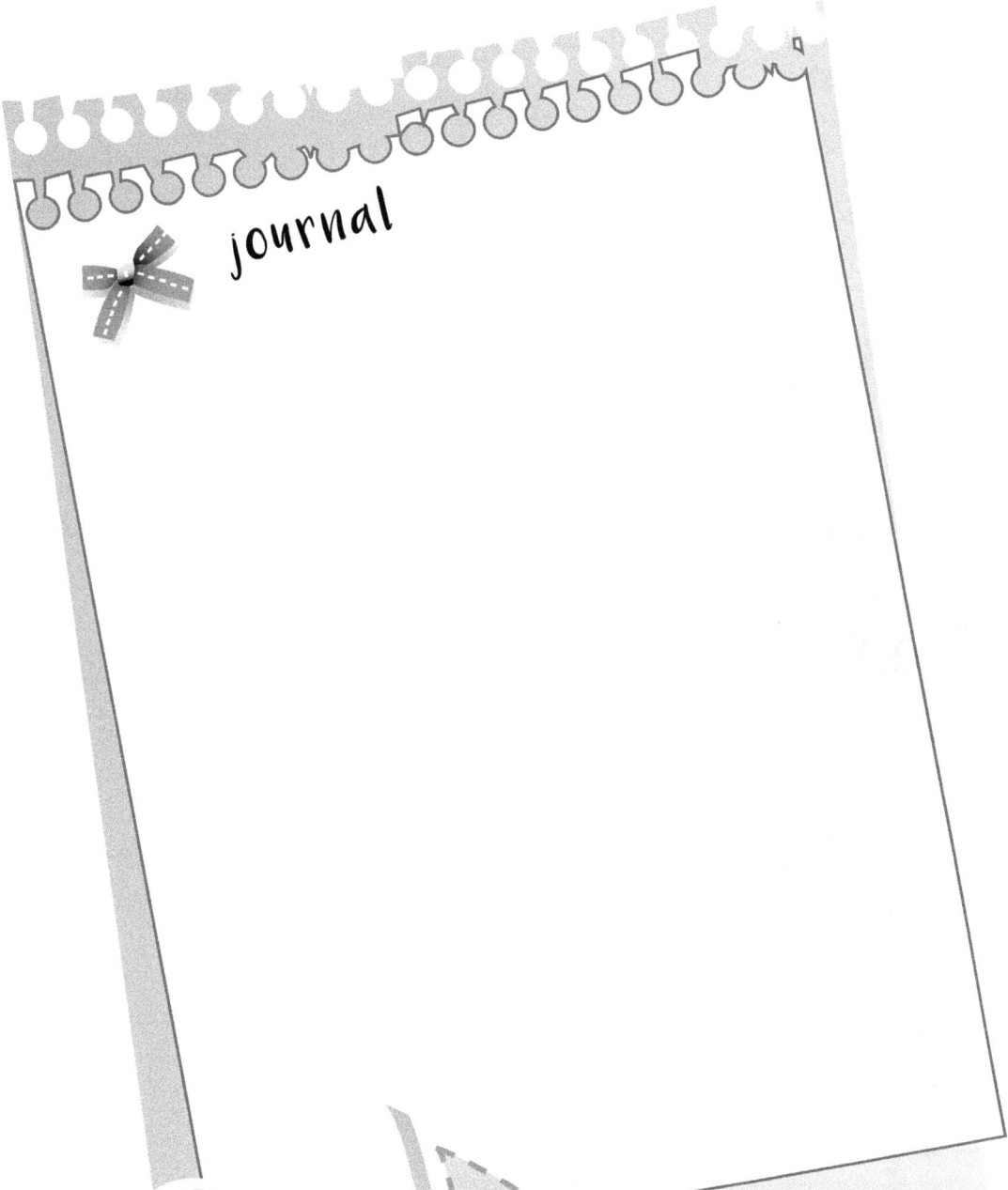

journal

Smile

CHEER
UP

nothing is
impossible

Dream
Big!

Quotes

Thoughts to ponder

notes:

journal

Smile

CHEER UP

nothing is impossible

Dream Big!

Quotes

Thoughts to ponder

notes:

journal

Smile

CHEER UP

nothing is impossible

Dream Big!

notes

Thoughts to ponder

notes:

journal

Smile

CHEER UP

nothing is impossible

Dream Big!

notes

Thoughts to ponder

notes:

 journal

 Smile

 CHEER UP

 nothing is impossible

 Dream Big!

Quotes

Thoughts to ponder

notes:

journal

Smile

nothing is impossible

Dream Big!

notes

Thoughts to ponder

notes:

journal

Smile

CHEER
UP

nothing is impossible

Dream Big!

Quotes

Thoughts to ponder

notes:

journal

Smile

CHEER

UP

nothing is impossible

Dream
Big!

Quotes

Thoughts to ponder

notes:

journal

Smile

CHEER UP

nothing is impossible

Dream Big!

notes

Thoughts to ponder

notes:

journal

Smile

nothing is impossible

Dream Big!

Quotes

Thoughts to ponder

notes:

journal

Smile

nothing is impossible

Dream Big!

Quotes

Thoughts to ponder

notes:

journal

Smile

CHEER
UP

nothing is impossible

Dream Big!

Notes

Thoughts to ponder

notes:

journal

Smile

CHEER
UP

nothing is impossible

Dream
Big!

Quotes

Thoughts to ponder

notes:

journal

Smile

CHEER UP

nothing is impossible

Dream Big!

Quotes

Thoughts to ponder

notes:

journal

Smile

nothing is impossible

Dream Big!

Quotes

Thoughts to ponder

notes:

journal

Smile

CHEER UP

nothing is impossible

Dream Big!

Quotes

Thoughts to ponder

notes:

journal

Smile

CHEER UP

nothing is impossible

Dream Big!

Quotes

Thoughts to ponder

notes:

journal

Smile

CHEER UP

nothing is impossible

Dream Big!

Quotes

Thoughts to ponder

notes:

journal

Smile

CHEER
UP

nothing is impossible

Dream Big!

Quotes

Thoughts to ponder

notes:

journal

Smile

nothing is impossible

Dream Big!

CHEER UP

Quotes

Thoughts to ponder

notes:

journal

Smile

nothing is impossible

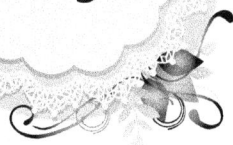

Dream Big!

www.ingramcontent.com/pod-product-compliance
Lightning Source LLC
Chambersburg PA
CBHW081334090426
42737CB00017B/3135